digital **delight**

Planning, measuring, and optimizing great digital customer and employee experiences

SECOND EDITION

by GREG KIHLSTRÖM

digital delight second edition | Greg Kihlström

Contents

About the Author 5

Acknowledgements 8

Introduction to the 2nd Edition 11

Introduction 14

Part 1: Plan 20

Part 2: Build 63

Part 3: Measure 120

Part 4: Optimize 155

Conclusion Digital delight 172

References 174

digital delight second edition | Greg Kihlström

Copyright © 2019 by Greg Kihlström.

All rights reserved. In accordance with the U.S. Copyright Act of 1976, the scanning, uploading, and electronic sharing of any part of this book without the permission of the publisher constitute unlawful piracy and theft of the author's intellectual property. If you would like to use material from the book (other than for review purposes), prior written must be obtained by contacting the author. Thank you for your support of the author's rights.

Published by:
The Agile World
3100 Clarendon Blvd, Suite 200
Arlington, VA 22201

First Edition: March 1, 2019
Second Edition: August 30, 2019

The publisher is not responsible for websites (or their content) that are not owned by the publisher.

Cover Design by Greg Kihlström
Edited by Janelle Kihlström

ISBN - 9781690018636

digital delight second edition | Greg Kihlström

FOR LINDSEY,
MY SOURCE OF CONTINUAL DELIGHT.

digital delight second edition | Greg Kihlström

About the Author

"Just because you can, doesn't mean you should."
-Greg Kihlström

Greg is a best-selling author, speaker, and entrepreneur, currently an advisor and consultant to top companies on customer experience, employee experience, and digital transformation initiatives as Principal and Chief Strategist at GK5A. He is also the host of The Agile Brand with Greg Kihlström podcast. He is a two-time CEO and Co-Founder, growing both companies organically and through acquisitions, and ultimately leading both to be acquired (one in 2017, and the other in 2021). As a strategist, digital transformation, and customer experience advisor, he has worked with some of the world's top brands, including Adidas, Choice

Hotels, Coca-Cola, Dell, FedEx, HP, Marriott, MTV, Starbucks, Toyota, and VMware.

He is a member of the School of Marketing Faculty at the Association of National Advertisers, and currently serves on the University of Richmond's Customer Experience Advisory Board and on the Workhouse Arts Foundation Board as Chair of the Marketing Special Committee. Greg was the founding Chair of the American Advertising Federation's National Innovation Committee, and served on the Virginia Tech Pamplin College of Business Marketing Mentorship Advisory Board. Greg is Lean Six Sigma Black Belt certified, is an Agile Certified Coach (ICP-ACC) and holds a certification in Business Agility (ICP-BAF).

Meaningful Measurement of the Customer Experience (2022), Greg's eighth and latest book provides guidance on how to create a customer-centric culture that prioritizes customer needs while aligning internal teams around a common goal. Greg's sixth book, The Center of Experience (2020) talks about how customer and employee experience can be operationalized into a cohesive brand experience. The Agile Brand (2018), follows the evolution of branding from its beginnings to the authentic relationship with brands that modern consumers want, and gives practical examples of what you can do to create a more modern, agile brand while staying true to your core values. His podcast, The Agile Brand with Greg Kihlström, launched in early 2019 and discusses brand strategy, marketing, and customer experience with some of the world's leading experts and leaders.

Greg is a contributing writer to Fast Company, Forbes, MarTech and CMSWire, and has been featured in publications such as Advertising Age and The Washington Post. Greg has been named a 2022 Top 10 Marketing and Customer Experience Thought Leader by Thinkers 360, was named one of ICMI's Top 25 CX Thought Leaders of 2022, and a DC Inno 50 on Fire winner as a DC trendsetter in Marketing. He's participated as a keynote speaker and panelist at industry events around the world including Internet Week New York, Internet Summit, DigiMarCon, Digital Summit, EventTech, MarTech, SMX Social Media, and

digital delight second edition | Greg Kihlström

VMworld. He has guest lectured at several colleges and universities including VCU Brandcenter, Georgetown University, Duke University, American University, University of Maryland, Howard University, and Virginia Tech.

digital delight second edition | Greg Kihlström

Acknowledgements

There are many people who make writing a book like this possible, and it's simply not possible to name them all. The team at Cravety—Ed Bodensiek, JG Staal, Rachael Satterfield, Mike Gardner, among others—is certainly a huge part of that and is part of my continual education about experience. As both customer and employee experience continue to evolve as a discipline, it's a truly interesting time to be working and innovating in our space.

I'd also like to thank my sister Janelle for editing this book and yet again displaying patience with first drafts of my writing. Thanks also to my wife Lindsey, who is always supportive of my late nights and long weekends writing and researching.

The Carousel30 team (who became Yes& after the acquisition) has also been a critical part of my growth in the discipline of experience.

digital delight second edition | Greg Kihlström

Finally, there are many others whose conversations, ideas, and presences in my life have contributed in some way to ideas or thoughts in this and other writing I've done. I fear I may leave someone out if I try to name them all.

digital delight second edition | Greg Kihlström

"What delights us in visible beauty is the invisible."
— *Marie von Ebner-Eschenbach*

Introduction to the 2nd Edition

> *"To win in the marketplace you must first win in the workplace."*
> —Doug Conant, CEO Campbell's Soup

I must confess that not a lot of time has gone by between the 1st and 2nd editions of this book. But perhaps that is a sign of our times that any book focused on the discipline of experience (or any field in a state of rapid growth) will have plenty to add to it after a short period of time.

The biggest change to this edition of the book is new content and insights on *employee* experience (EX), which has been an increasingly important component of not only my work but the experience industry in general. EX is the natural progression of experience, as it moves inward and more central to the enterprise. I'm proud to be actively working in this realm on a number of initiatives for forward-thinking companies, and thus some of the newer thoughts on experience in this book come directly from the work I've done in researching and practicing in the field of employee experience.

Creating a great employee experience is critical to organizations as they are in continual competition for talent, both from their established rivals, as well as other more innovative companies, or other modes of working. The gig economy has changed the employment landscape and puts traditional companies in competition with work that affords a more flexible lifestyle and different modes of working.

In a good economy, competition for talent amongst rivals is fierce. But even in a bad economy, competition between traditional *work* and gig economy work is also tough. The economic downturn in late 2008 helped to create what we now know of as the gig economy and gig work, and the world will never be the same.

Thus, employee experience isn't a trend, or a fad that is useful only during good times. Like *customer* experience, it is the new normal. Consumers are used to having personalized experiences everywhere they go. Since every employee is *also* someone's customer, they are also used to a focus on experience behing the norm. From Gen Z who is starting to enter the workforce, all the way to Boomers nearing retirement, we are living in an experience-focused world.

I wrote the contents of this book to help practictioners make sense of this and build digital components of experience in a more strategic and measurable way. I hope you enjoy!

digital delight second edition | Greg Kihlström

Introduction

> *"Customer service is part of a holistic customer experience that is capable of providing a critical competitive advantage in today's increasingly cluttered and commoditized marketplace."*
> *– Joseph Jaffe*

> *"Highly engaged employees make the customer experience. Disengaged employees break it."*
> *-Timothy R. Clark*

We are truly living in the age of experience.

Experience is every interaction that a person, whether a current or potential customer, a potential, current or past employee, or anyone else has with a brand.

I decided to call this book *digital delight* because most of what we'll be talking about on the pages that follow is the creation of both customer experience (CX) and employee experience (EX) that heavily lean on systems and measurements that are digitally-based.

Experience measurement isn't just about digital, however. While we live in an increasingly digital world, to truly measure CX and EX, we have to be able to measure both online and offline interactions. While we may use digital tools to do so, we can't ever forget that experience is wherever the customer or employee is, and whatever interaction they may be having. This would be an in-store conversation, a phone call to customer services, or, yes, a website or social media interaction.

With the proliferation of tools that allow better and more holistic design of customer experience and consumer journeys, comes an increased ability to measure, analyze, and optimize.

Think about the business impacts that the quality of your customer service affects. Things like revenue, cost to serve, profitability, and even employee satisfaction can be closely tied to CX or EX performance.

Customer experience and employee experience performance also influences behavioral outcomes such as (in the case of customers) buying, buying again, buying more, recommending to friends and other activities critical to an organization's bottom line, or (in the case of employees) accepting an offer, staying with a company, and actively contributing as an employee.

Delight is the ultimate goal

While the indicators of a great customer experience are things like retention, customer lifetime value, and marketing campaign success, the ultimate goal is to delight customers.

Because where there are delighted customers, there are all sorts of benefits. Delighted consumers buy more, spend more time-consuming information, tell more of their friends and colleagues, and are overall more valuable customers and brand advocates.

And while "delight" may seem aspirational to some, it should always be the ultimate goal of any customer experience effort.

The purpose of this book

This book was written to help CX and EX practitioners, particularly those newer to the discipline, and those whose jobs (such as marketers or human resources professionals) are more consistently overlapping with those who might have been working in customer or employee experience for years. The goal of this book is to help plan, measure and optimize digital customer experience and employee experience systems.

While we will reference customer experience (CX) and employee experience (EX) often in this book, it is not my intention that this serve as a standalone reference of CX and EX best practices. Its sole focus is on providing guidance for planning, measuring, and optimizing experience systems. The actual execution of experience is a more than worthy subject, but not what I've focused on with this book.

digital delight second edition | Greg Kihlström

This book is divided into four primary sections, that each discuss a key component of a high-performing experience for customers or employees:

- Plan
- Build
- Measure
- Optimize

Within each section we will explore from both the CX and EX perspective. Because the first edition of this book spent more of its focus on customers and customer experience, you may notice that many examples come from the CX world. Keep in mind that a lot of what has been done in customer experience can be adapted (with some obvious and some not-so-obvious changes) to the employee experience world.

While CX and EX are very different from one another in *practice*, a lot of the principles behind planning and measuring them are not. Thus, think of this book as a guide to the methodologies and thinking behind designing experience systems for either, and not as a prescriptive how-to guide. For that, we'd also have to look a lot more detailed by industry, step in the journey, and one book of this size couldn't do justice to both CX and EX.

For instance, within employee experience, there is a large difference between retail organizations with hourly workers dealing directly with consumers, and professional services organizations with primarily salaried employees working in a B2B environment.

So instead, we're going to stick with the fundamentals of setting up an experience system at an organization.

Let's get started!

Part 1: Plan

> "Customer service is the experience we deliver to our customer. It's the promise we keep to the customer. It's how we follow through for the customer. It's how we make them feel when they do business with us."
>
> – Shep Hyken

chapter 1.1
Creating delight

"You've got to start with the customer experience and work back toward the technology, not the other way around."
– Steve Jobs

There is a plethora of materials already on the subject of experience. In my work, I've helped clients with customer experience, employee experience, even *student* experience. This work is a natural outcome of several other disciplines. On the customer side, there is branding, marketing, customer service, and product development (among others). On the employee side, there is human resources, talent branding, and information technology (IT). Experience touches everyone, and thus it requires a cross-disciplinary approach in order to really get it right.

Great experience translates into many things: happier employees who stay in an organization longer while being more productive, happier customers who buy more products or services and who tell others they should buy even more. These are a couple examples but there are many more, and increased product sales, and employee retention are realistic outcomes of improving experience.

What about *delight?* On one hand, it seems like a strong term to use when the service you sell might be rather mundane. Is it possible to delight a B2B customer who is purchasing a rather commoditized service?

You can probably guess my answer to this, because I wouldn't have written a book called *digital delight* if I didn't believe that this is possible in many situations.

Delight isn't always about the product itself, but it can be about the way the process of acquiring it made you feel. Or maybe it's the relief of knowing that when you have to call to get help or return the product, the process was built around helping you solve a challenge and not to save money for a department within a company.

Delight can be big, or it can be very small. The surprise when something is easier than it used to be, or than it was at the last company you worked with. Or the feeling you get when you got more than you thought you would receive.

Delight can be fleeting, or it can leave a lasting impression. While we can sometimes take personalized experiences for granted, companies can still go the extra mile to put themselves in our shoes and give us something we never thought to ask about.

Or as an employee, delight can be knowing there is flexibility to, as a parent, take the time you need to with your children, or learn more about a field you have an intellectual interest in. As we'll discuss later in the book, employees can only be motivated so much by money or other superficial perks. Finding ways to delight your employees means you can keep them engaged and motivated without continually throwing money at the issue.

Delight can be digital, or it can be analog or IRL (in the real world). While the scope of this book is mostly within the digital realm, don't relegate your thinking to only what can be achieved digitally.

Finally, delight can be spontaneous, or it can be designed as part of a holistic experience. We're going to discuss the latter in depth in the pages that follow. While spontaneous events are great, truly successful company cultures for employees and customer experiences for consumers are the product of a good amount of intention. This includes the design, planning, implementation, and optimization we will discuss in this book.

chapter 1.2
Great experience starts with design thinking

"When the customer comes first, the customer will last."
– Robert Half

A great amount of time and investment is spent ensuring that consumers move through a sales funnel in the way that creates the desired outcome for marketers. What we know, however, is that consumers are not always likely to have a linear progression from the point of awareness to the point of sale.

Thus, more effort is now put into looking at the holistic customer experience. Customers are increasingly device-agnostic, switching between devices during the course of the day. They most often prefer customer service messages to be sent to their mobile phone (registration required) and are likely to perform comparison shopping before deciding to make a purchase in-store or online.

Because of these behaviors, you have a continually disrupted customer experience, not a smooth, linear progression from initial contact to sale.

Likewise, employee experience faces similar challenges. Employees with 9 to 5 jobs spend their nights and weekends being consumers and are used to behaving in a specific way given that fact. Thus, if they get to work and are forced to use a device that feels foreign to them, or have other negative experiences, they are likely to do one of several things (or all the above):

- Complain on social media sites like Glassdoor, hurting the employer's chances of hiring great talent in the future
- Quit the company, thus causing their employer to pay the cost of replacing them
- Stay at the company but become less productive, thus costing their employer lost opportunity

Optimizing touch points individually is not the answer

Too often, those charged with designing and owning experience focus on individual channels or tactics, such as (in the case of CX) in-store experience, social media, email or the company's website. While any of these individual experiences may be great on their own, as McKinsey states, "Individual touchpoints may perform well even if the overall experience is poor."

While the dawn of big data made it much easier to monitor and analyze your marketing channels, many marketers still do not have a comprehensive view of how the overall customer experience is performing. In addition, the existing customer experience is often a legacy of systems and processes set up over the preceding decades, meaning that marketers are optimizing channels with the assumptions that the customer experiences they've inherited are as efficient as they can be.

When approaching CX, my agency approaches our engagements with clients by starting with an analysis of the customer experience and, where possible, design solutions around the customer first, instead of the other way around. By prioritizing the customer journey, we achieve more successful outcomes, including better long-term engagement and lifetime value.

Employee experience engagements are approached similarly, with organizational culture assessments, employee motivation assessments, and an overall experience maturity assessment that first sets a baseline. We then work with HR, internal communications, Technology, and other stakeholders to identify and prioritize points along the employee journey that will enhance engagement, retention, and productivity.

Enter design thinking

At best, each channel has been optimized as much as possible. But what could be possible if the entire system were re-imagined? When you have optimized silos that your customer accesses and still don't have great customer experience results, I believe this is when design thinking should enter the discussion.

For those unfamiliar with the term "design thinking," it has origins beginning as early as the 1950s, particularly in architecture and other design-related fields. Since then, the concept has been adopted and more popularized by David M. Kelley, founder of IDEO[1]. Design thinking is the philosophy that problems can be solved through creating solutions around customer needs without assuming existing structures, systems or processes need to exist. This is in contrast to creating solutions based on a company's desired outcomes.

In many ways, this would seem to be the antithesis of the analysis-based agile marketing approach many marketers take, relying heavily on data and optimizing channels based on past interactions.

When done well, design thinking has the power to disrupt markets. From my perspective, this is because it doesn't assume that the existing systems and processes many consumers have grown used to (but actively dislike) need to exist.

For instance, Airbnb has taken a customer-centric view of the hospitality industry that doesn't assume hotels and the traditional hotel-booking structure need to exist. Instead, it matches people and the things they need with other individuals who can provide that service. This type of thinking has the power to disrupt any industry.

Agile marketing and design thinking work together for CX and EX success.

Thus, rather than being mutually exclusive, design thinking and agile marketing go hand-in-hand to create a great customer experience. Design thinking provides the foundation, and the data analysis inherent in agile marketing provides the continuous improvement and enhancement.

Tom Ritchey describes this in detail using the terms "analysis" and "synthesis" as a way of creating successful outcomes through both a subtractive (analysis) and additive (synthesis) process — much like using agile marketing (analysis) and design thinking (synthesis) together to solve customer experience challenges[2].

Brands that combine these two approaches can find success well beyond others that simply take their legacy models for granted.

For instance, Capital One has been extremely successful in reinventing itself from a traditional financial institution into a design-driven company with financial products. Its investments in digital design and product development teams have paid off by setting its customer experience apart from its larger (and smaller) competitors in a very crowded marketplace where product benefits are difficult to distinguish.

Of course, simply starting with great design isn't enough. Continual monitoring and optimization of the customer experience across all channels are essential for brands. This is where agile marketing and design thinking intersect and work together in a way that benefits both customers and the brands alike.

Chapter 1.3
The intersection of CX and EX

> *"Always treat your employees exactly as you want them to treat your best customers."*
>
> *Stephen R. Covey*

Successful companies have always understood that happy customers buy more, buy more often, and are most likely to recommend others to buy as well. They also understand the happy employees stay longer at a company (which costs a company less money over time), are generally more productive, and contribute to creating happier customers.

This means that customer experience (CX) and employee experience (EX) have a lot to do with one another. Let's explore three ways that customer experience and employee experience intersect and can work together.

Feedback is best when timely and relevant

Making sure the employees get to see customer feedback where and when they can take the most action. This means having the tools and methods to both listen for both internal and external feedback, as well as the processes and discipline to review and respond.

Listening to customer feedback is critical to understanding both what they love as well as what they wish were improved. But it's not enough to simply listen. You need systems and processes in place to not only collect the information, but do something meaningful with it. When I work with brands, I make sure to understand what silos or bottlenecks might be getting in the way of the right information getting to the best place.

When you actively listen to employee feedback, it empowers employees to be able to make the type of changes in the organization that keeps them both productive and happy, and can lower attrition. The best part of this is that companies with satisfied employees often have an easier time creating satisfied customers.

Both customers and employees love rewards

One point of commonality between both happy employees and loyal customers is that they feel loved and rewarded. Whether this is through personalized customer experiences or meaningful recognition at the employee level, both are valued and valuable to an organization.

In fact, this is definitely a case where the methods and tactics used to reward each group (customers or employees) will vary greatly, but the fact remains that employees who feel valued contribute to making customers who feel valued.

It is also important to understand is that the same time of incentives and rewards don't even make all your employees more engaged or happier in their jobs. Make sure to keep in mind that everyone is different and is motivated by different things. When I work with a client on CX or EX (or both), I always make sure to emphasize that successful implementation isn't a one-size-fits-all approach. You need to make sure to account for a variety of tastes and motivators.

Experience is everything, and everything is experience

Let's end with perhaps the most obvious, but also the most inclusive tie-in between employee and customer experience. Not only is experience worth a lot to both employees and customers, both audiences consider experience to be a combination of *everything* they experience.

This means that focusing on having a really good experience part of the time, or on a few channels isn't enough. Your customers have grown device-agnostic and rarely use a single device to communicate with you. They don't care that your website gives a phenomenal user experience, if they try to call someone on the phone and are treated rudely.

The same goes with employees. The employee experience starts from before their first day and extends throughout the employment, including their last day at work. Companies that embrace CX and EX understand that the details matter, and that every moment helps make up an overall experience.

Understanding the important link between customer experience and employee experience can give brands an important competitive advantage in a crowded marketplace. Focusing on both ends of the experience is a win-win for all.

digital delight second edition | Greg Kihlström

chapter 1.4
Calculating the value of CX & EX

> *"It is not the employer who pays the wages. Employers only handle the money ... It is the customer who pays the wages."*
> *– Henry Ford*

It is well understood that the better the data you have, the better the decisions you can make. For larger organizations with a lot of legacy infrastructure, this can require a lot of integration between systems and creating feedback mechanisms that tie everything together. The benefits of this can be dramatic, however. Or, as David Linthicum, chief cloud strategy officer at

Deloitte Consulting, puts it in an article on Informatica, the value of data integration is "access to near perfect information," since you finally have a full view of what is happening across the landscape of your customer and employee experiences[3].

To do this well, it is not only about integrating your marketing and communications in the case of customers, or your HR systems for employee experience. You also need to think about what happens after a sale. How do you communicate new messages and updates to current customers? Just as importantly, how does a customer communicate with you for support and other questions?

Experience is defined as every touch point someone can have with your brand. Unless you're able to calculate the value of each of those, you are missing out on critical data. For CX, Customer journey orchestration helps solve this challenge in a meaningful way.

This chapter is going to focus primarily on customer experience and the customer journey, though there are several points that can be applied to employee experience as well.

What customer journey orchestration does

Customer journey orchestration ties each touch point a customer can have with you and the related measurements and data sources so that all of your systems and marketing channels talk with one another and ensure your customers are getting the information they need.

But simply talking isn't enough. Remember, all of this orchestration can happen several times a minute, and in some cases, in a nearly infinite variety of combinations of entry points, requests and customer needs. As important as the data integration component is, it's also helpful to use artificial intelligence to ensure the correct actions are being taken at the right time, at a rate no human could keep up with and that simple segmentation tools are not built to handle.

To gain a better understanding of the value of orchestrating your customer experience, let's explore a few concepts you're likely familiar with, but through a new lens.

Cost per acquisition, customer lifetime value, and expected value

Understanding what it takes to win a new customer is critical. This is a combination of marketing and advertising costs, plus any sales costs, divided by the number of new customers acquired during that period. This is commonly called cost per acquisition (CPA). Most marketers already understand this well.

The downside with only looking at CPA is that you are evaluating things after they happen instead of being able to anticipate and adjust in real-time. You can see that a customer cost you $10.25 to acquire, but only after they made a purchase. What if another customer cost you $50 to acquire, and your optimal price point for the product you're selling is $39.99? You might have technically made an acquisition, but no profit was made because you spent too much trying to acquire them.

More important than cost per acquisition, however, is the total value of a consumer over time. This is most often referred to as customer lifetime value (CLV). This factors into not only the initial cost per customer but the projected (or actual) value over time.

If you go back to the initial scenario of the customer who cost $50 to acquire and look at CLV, you might have a different view. What if you knew that if you could get this customer to switch to your brand, you'd have a customer for life because they met the criteria for loyalty for your brand and posed little risk of switching back? In that case, you might be willing to spend $100 to acquire them as long as you have a plan to activate them over their lifetime. While this is not a groundbreaking concept, the ability to embrace this idea becomes easier for most marketers when you introduce customer journey orchestration driven by artificial intelligence.

The expected value, or expected CLV, is a way of predicting customer lifetime value before the end of the customer's journey. This is something that can be predicted using past activity or behavioral models from similar personas and other methods that use artificial intelligence, or machine learning, to get more accurate over time.

By incorporating expected CLV, you can overcome the issue of just looking backward. You can predict whether or not an individual is worth spending $50 or even $100 on in the first place, or if you should move on because you're unlikely to make your investment back on them.

This can also drive the messages and channels you use, as well as the offers and even the incentives you show consumers. After all, why would you want to show a risky customer your best offer when there's a low likelihood of making your cost per acquisition back?

Benefits of orchestration

By using a customer journey orchestration framework and tools, you can more easily sync data between systems, see the points in your customer experience that are inefficient or ineffective and measure the value and risk each step of the way. Additionally, with behavioral modeling and machine learning, the system becomes smarter and better at what it does with the more data you feed it. This means it will provide a better return on investment the more you use it.

While some organizations may face an uphill battle to fully implement something like this across their entire customer experience, even starting small across certain segments or areas can be a good way to start.

What value do you place on having the most "perfect information" possible? When it allows you to target the right customer, at the right time, with the best message, the results can be well worth it.

chapter 1.5
Understanding the voice of the customer (VOC)

"Your most unhappy customers are your greatest source of learning." – Bill Gates

A key aspect of optimizing your customer experience is creating a consumer-centric mindset both in your organization and throughout the buying process. Doing this well requires listening to the way consumers are talking about your brand and its products or services, as well as their needs and requirements, commonly referred to as the voice of the customer, or VOC.

In order to better understand how to use VOC and the types of feedback that your customers are providing, let's divide it into three unique aspects, each with their own distinct attributes and value to an organization. In the work I do with clients, all three of these facets are used to form a cohesive picture of what a customer needs, what their experience has been and how they are feeling about a brand.

Keep in mind that similar approaches can be taken for employees and the employee experience by listening to the Voice of the Employee (VoE). While this chapter speaks primarily in terms of customer experience, there are many lessons that can be applied to EX here.

Explicit feedback

This is information and feedback that an organization gathers directly from a customer and is explicitly related to their experience. Common examples of this would be surveys or other research, as well as complaints or other feedback logged through customer service channels. Net Promoter Score (NPS) might be the most common implementation of an explicit feedback mechanism. In employee experience we often refer to the Employee Net Promoter Score (eNPS) which functions similarly.

This type of feedback is valuable because you are able to directly collect this and, because of that, it's the type that you have the most control over. Because you have the most control over it, it's also the easiest to tie back to a specific customer as well.

Using explicit feedback, such as a Net Promoter Score, can help you assess how your customer experience efforts are performing over time. This can help you shape policies, programs and even how you train your employees. Other methods can yield more immediate results. For instance, surveys within your website can gather direct feedback on the shopping experience so that you can see how new changes are affecting people's attitudes about choosing your brand.

Indirect feedback

This type of feedback is information that customers provide and/or are gathered by third-party channels, which includes a wide variety of platforms and channels. These could range from review sites like Yelp to social media comments and sentiment, or even conversational anecdotes shared during customer service calls or chats.

My agency looks at a lot of indirect feedback from channels such as social media to determine how current or potential customers are reacting to our clients' products and services. Using monitoring tools, we're able to track consumer sentiment about products or trends in the market.

This type of feedback is valuable because consumers often speak differently and are more open and honest when they are in what they perceive to be a neutral place. For instance, they may not share the full extent of their frustration directly with a customer service representative if they are concerned it might negatively impact their relationship or account. They may, however, share this with their friends and family on social media or on an online forum where they feel there is more free discussion and there are others who feel the same way. While this can often be negative feedback, there are typically plenty of positive discussions as well.

It's important to know when to sit back and listen, and when to engage when consumers are discussing your brand. Sometimes, it's better to observe and find ways to incorporate indirect feedback into your actions rather than try to explain your decisions. You shouldn't appear defensive when explaining your positions. If you participate in conversations, it should be to add value or additional information, not just try to make your brand look good.

Implicit feedback

This type of VOC feedback is not explicit and must be inferred based on things that you can measure. This is usually data that is related to a customer journey or history that relates to performance or how well a process or system works over time. Unlike explicit feedback, where the metrics are direct and specific, implicit feedback would include things like how long it takes a customer to complete a process or the number of steps it takes them to successfully complete an e-commerce checkout. Implicit feedback generally involves measuring a process that involves several steps and potentially crosses several channels.

This type of feedback is valuable because it often looks more holistically at the customer experience, or at least an entire step in a larger process, as opposed to explicit feedback, which is often looking at a single data point without a lot of background or reference.

Implicit feedback offers a great opportunity to look at the big picture and optimize. For instance, if you see that the drop-off during your e-commerce checkout process is increasing over time, you have an issue that can be addressed. Take small steps to optimize this. For instance, you could shorten unnecessary fields in a form, decrease the number of steps and then see what the effect is on those actions.

Using each facet's unique benefits, you can get better insights and understandings and find ways to improve processes, messaging and measurement.

digital delight second edition | Greg Kihlström

chapter 1.6
Personalization strategy to win CX

"Get closer than ever to your customers. So close that you tell them what they need well before they realize it themselves."
– Steve Jobs

Please note that while this chapter focuses on personalization and the customer experience, we'll discuss the employee experience in the next chapter.

We've been hearing about the benefits of personalization for years now. Consumers, bombarded with marketing and advertising from the moment they wake up to the moment they drift off staring at their smartphones, are demanding tailored experiences, products and offers from the brands they support.

A recent survey by Segment revealed that nearly half of all shoppers made impulse buys from personalized recommendations, and nearly three-quarters show frustration when they do not experience some type of personalization[4].

Additionally, 44% of consumers will become repeat buyers if they have a personalized shopping experience. Personalization is certainly not a new thing, though many organizations large and small are struggling to implement it in meaningful ways. We're going to explore four initial steps that will help you get your organization ready to take advantage of the myriad of opportunities that personalization provides.

Ask the right questions

As with any strategic challenge, it all begins with a simple question: What is the problem you're trying to solve? Many times, personalization is allowing your customers to more clearly understand how your product or service is relevant to them. Perhaps you have so many products and services, it's hard for customers to understand which ones are the best fit. This leads many to leave your store (or website) before they can make a decision. Maybe your marketplace is flooded with competitors and your products fill a niche that can be difficult to explain without understanding who they are first.

Understanding what problems you want the personalization to help solve will narrow the scope of your efforts, help you set the important key performance indicators (KPIs) to measure them, and will help you sharpen your focus on where, how and with whom you want to begin.

Know your audiences

Once you get the important questions answered that drive the goals of your personalization efforts, it's time to ask another key question: Who are we tailoring our content for?

Typical website design and development projects require the creation of personas, or typical users, that will interact with the site. These are based on target audiences. Creating an identifiable person helps to make the user experience design a little more real.

The same approach to understanding your customers is needed when planning personalization, whether it is solely on a website or across your complete customer experience. Following a user through their experience and understanding the typical questions, problems or needs they might have will help you to better understand how to use personalization.

Content (strategy) is king

You can't have personalization without the content that is tailored to the individuals. Many times, this is a stumbling block for organizations that seemingly want an ambitiously robust program. They fail to understand that for each variation that is personalized, they need to define and find a method to create the content assets to display.

The best way to understand how diverse your content creation will need to be is to create a content map that contains the universe of options available. This map should encompass the entirety of the customer experience. It should outline the personas you are reaching, the content categories (e.g., product types, industry verticals) that comprise your products and services, the places your customers are encountering them (e.g., website, email, in-store) and the mediums (e.g., imagery, text descriptions, videos) in which you need to display personalized information.

Be realistic

While there are certainly a lot of tools available for personalization and endless possibilities to customize experiences, it's important to start your personalization efforts like you would any other marketing effort.

Being realistic means starting your efforts in a manageable way, testing your efforts, then optimizing them over time. While you may want every touchpoint in your customer experience to have some method of personalization, the only way to truly understand the effectiveness of what you are doing is to make sure there is a good test for each.

It is also important to understand the breadth and depth of where and how personalization will occur. Will it only exist on your website? What about your brick-and-mortar store, mobile app, customer service, email marketing or advertising?

Finally, you need to understand the tools you need to have at your disposal. Make sure you understand how you are tracking your customers as they interact with your brand using different devices and methods throughout the day.

Implementing a successful personalization strategy is not easy, but by following a few proven steps, you can focus your efforts to be successful. Even Amazon, a clear leader in this approach since it first started showing product recommendations many years ago, was much less sophisticated when it first launched this feature compared to where it is today. Understanding that you don't have to do everything at once can help you prioritize your efforts, while you keep the big picture in mind.

The most successful personalization solves a real challenge that your customers have and demonstrates that your products or services are the ideal fit. By following this approach, you'll find providing personalization make happy, long-term customers.

chapter 1.7
Personalization & the employee experience

"Employees who believe that management is concerned about them as a whole person – not just an employee – are more productive, more satisfied, more fulfilled. Satisfied employees mean satisfied customers, which leads to profitability."
- Anne M. Mulcahy, former CEO of Xerox

While we spent the previous chapter discussing personalization for *customers*, it's also important to talk about how we can personalize for employees as well.

Marketers spend a good deal of effort trying to learn more about consumers who visit their websites and interact with their marketing efforts. This takes a lot of art and science to piece together. But think for a minute how this becomes dramatically easier when dealing with employees.

After all, employers know almost everything about their employees, from exactly where they live, their demographics, to their *social security number,* even!

In addition, every employee is also a consumer. Guaranteed. Thus, they are used to having personalized experience outside of work and many (particularly digital natives belonging to younger generations) *assume* customized experiences will exist already. It's not even a matter of delighting at this point, but rather meeting baseline expectations.

Given all this, why wouldn't employers find ways to personalize the employee experience? Let's look at a couple ways to do this digitally.

Content

The natural way to personalize for the employee is to do so with content. Just like you would personalize a customer-facing website for consumers, you can personalize intranet content, internal newsletters, and other communications.

This could make the difference between some great engagement with some important communications, and the employee ignoring "generic" corporate messaging.

Opportunities

Let's take this a step further beyond content display. If you know an employee's interests, their role, and potentially what motivates them, you can go beyond showing weather near where their house is located. Instead, you can provide tailored programs, learning opportunities, mentoring meetups, and more that can offer some true employee engagement.

I'm proud to be working on an initiative now that deals with employees and their true, intrinsic motivations. By looking at what engages someone, beyond salary bumps and foosball tables, employers can truly get next-level work out from their workforce, and employees can be happier and feel more fulfilled from how they spend their days. A true win-win situation!

These are just a couple ideas of what can be done when you start putting employees at the center of how you design communications and growth opportunities.

digital delight second edition | Greg Kihlström

Part 2: Build

"Make the customer the hero of your story."
– Ann Handley

"Highly engaged employees make the customer experience. Disengaged employees break it."
– Timothy R. Clark

chapter 2.1
Orchestrating a better CX or EX

"Everything starts with the customer"
– Louis XIV

Playing a piece of music well takes a lot of coordination, skill at playing the instruments involved and an underlying sense of rhythm to tie it all together. Richard Wagner, the famous conductor and composer, once said, "The whole duty of a conductor is comprised in his ability always to indicate the right tempo." While the conductor can't play all the instruments in a symphony themselves, they are critical to making sure the right notes are played at the right time.

This strategy needs to guide everything we do, starting with the individual you are designing an experience around. But along the way, we often get tangled up in the "notes," the tactics they are executing or even individual data points they are collecting and measuring against.

As valuable as the individual touchpoints you have with your customers or employees may be, do you have a "conductor" who is able to make sure all your channels, applications and systems are all playing to the same tempo?

Some of this can and should be done by a human being. But with so many automated systems and integrations needed in the modern customer and employee experience, it can be impossible for even a team of people to keep up with it all.

Orchestration between channels and experiences requires a conductor whose technique is as sophisticated as the steps and sequence of your journey.

Let's take a look at experience orchestration and what it means to today's marketer, HR practitioner, and others within your organization.

Mapping the experience

In the rest of this chapter, we're going to talk primarily about the customer experience, but keep in mind that the process and steps in orchestration are similar whether you are designing around employees or customers.

The first step in orchestration is understanding the full extent of your customer journey. Most likely you have mapped this out in some form or other, but if you haven't, there's no time like the present. Think through all of the touch points your potential, current and recurring customers have with you. This could be online, in a store, on the phone or any number of places where an advertisement might be placed.

It is critical to map not only the ideal scenario — a customer moving in a straight line from initial awareness to purchase — but also some less ideal scenarios, where a website visitor might bounce from the site after clicking on a paid social ad. Including your methods for bringing them back, such as retargeting, is as critical as mapping the quickest route to a conversion. This will help you orchestrate a customer journey that has multiple roads to success.

Mind the gaps

Once you have a full accounting of the times and places consumers are interacting with your brand, it's time to understand and create solutions for how to move them from one point in the journey to the next.

For instance, if they are in the initial "awareness" phase of the buying journey and are still trying to understand the problem they need to solve, but they aren't ready to make a purchase, how do you make sure you provide them with more information that will educate them without being too aggressive with your sales tactics?

Choosing the right tactic at the right time is critical. For instance, if you are a business-to-business marketer in the above scenario, you might want to retarget that person with a white paper or other helpful content. You wouldn't want to jump right to closing a deal before you've demonstrated your value.

If a customer is further along in the buying journey and wants to buy sneakers, if they add something to their cart and then close their browser window, you know they had intent to buy. How many times have you received emails, Facebook ads or other retargeted ads if you did this while shopping? This is a rather simple example of automation, but it's still effective. Even more effective is to take the same approach at every step in your journey.

How good is your conductor?

The question here is, how good is your conductor? Is it smart enough to show the right message — on the right channel — to the right person throughout your entire customer experience? Or is it a one-size-fits-all approach? Finally, how does your conductor "talk" to all the different channels and platforms you use to reach your customers?

Another important thing to keep in mind when orchestrating your customer journey is to try to be platform-agnostic when possible and understand that your existing channels and infrastructure may need to undergo shifts. This could be due to new social channels popping up, changing analytics platforms, launching a new website, or any of the other many changes that might need to occur.

While some of these things may be necessary, they shouldn't completely disrupt the automation, measurement and management of your customer experience. For instance, my agency uses a tool with our clients to help them integrate with existing systems and allow them to talk with one another.

A great customer experience requires a smart strategy that understands consumer behavior and how your brand can meet people's needs at every stage of the journey. It also demands an integrated infrastructure, data sets and marketing systems that are playing the same tune.

When designing a great employee experience, you are going to have a different suite or tools and systems that are needed in order to be successful. Everything from HRIS systems, to budgeting, to mobile device management and many more will need to be coordinated at various places in the employee journey. But the same principles and ideas apply in how to do it well.

Chapter 2.2
Using Journey Orchestration and AI to Optimize CX

"Don't try to tell the customer what he wants. If you want to be smart, be smart in the shower. Then get out, go to work, and serve the customer!"
—Gene Buckley

A stellar customer experience requires a lot of pieces to be in place that span the internal-facing and external-facing parts of your organization.

Customer journey orchestration allows marketers to integrate different marketing technology systems and platforms together. For instance, you can tie together your social media advertising, your website, your email marketing, and your CRM or customer database. This means you can share information between them that helps each platform take the best actions based on the specific customer or their last actions.

Artificial intelligence will provide additional benefits. By creating a machine learning model, we will be able to observe and learn what customer interactions and behaviors create the most valuable customers. For instance, if we're able to observe and measure how customers behave when traveling between marketing platforms, and how they respond to different messaging using A/B testing, we can then "learn" how to optimize pathways. AI helps us automate this and show the best messages to the right customers and more. AI will also allow us to improve our results each time a user goes through the journey because our system gets better and learns what works (and what doesn't) each time.

In my experience, it's best to start initiatives like this with a "pilot project." Why a pilot project instead of a full-blown implementation? It minimizes risk and cost by getting you quicker results.

Determine your goals

As with any initiative at your organization, it is critical for all involved to have a clear understanding of expectations and measures of success. You should start with the big goals of how you want to measure the value of customers and the customer experience, and then drill down to something more specific and immediately actionable. It would be best to start with a smaller series of actions that can then be turned into our pilot project.

For instance, your overall goals might be to sell a product such as watches or clothing across a wide variety of marketing channels, and then turn those customers into referrers and repeat buyers. While this is the ultimate end goal, let's base our pilot project on something more focused. Why don't we focus on increasing the amount of product views from social media advertising?

Choose the right tools

In order to implement your pilot project, you'll need to put the right tools in place.

There are several customer journey orchestration tools available, and you will want to evaluate several before picking one. In my experience, the best choice comes down to a combination of its flexibility, price, and the technical knowledge level of those who will need to implement it.

For the artificial intelligence component of this, you will need to rely on either an inhouse data science team or an external consultant to write an application that is able to take in data from your marketing channels, and then assign a score to each interaction. For instance, a customer who goes from a Facebook ad and views 3 products on your website might get a score of 10, while a customer who only views 1 product on your website might get a score of 5. After you get enough data, you'll be able to start seeing which messages and audiences make up the most valuable customers.

Start with a pilot project

At this point, we've defined our goals and the tools we will use to create our pilot project. Now it's time to connect the dots. You'll need to connect your customer journey orchestration tool via its application programming interface (API) to your marketing platforms, which for the purpose of this pilot project include a social media advertising platform such as Facebook, your website, and your analytics.

You will also want to define the parameters you want to test and learn more about. I suggest using 2 dimensions: different messaging variations that can be tested via A/B testing, and different audience segments, which will be determined based on your target audience. For instance, you might want to test different messaging with different age groups, or perhaps based on people who live in urban versus suburban locations.

In addition, you will connect your artificial intelligence application to all of these so that you can measure and analyze what is happening and learn over time which messaging and approach works best. Once all of these are connected, you're ready to run the pilot!

Test, analyze and plan to expand

The learning and results from your pilot project will be a phenomenal way to determine what your next steps should be. Some questions to ask as you test and analyze are the following:

- Did you meet the goals you set for the project?
- Are there any gaps on your internal team that would be helpful for next time?
- What resources would be required to scale your pilot project enterprise-wide?
- Is it worth investing more in this project or is there another area or application that might be a better fit?

In the case of our pilot project, by connecting our customer journey orchestration tool with our marketing technology platforms and analytics, we will be able to see how it is performing in several different dimensions. Ultimately, if the goal of our pilot project is to get more views of our products, we can see if there was an uptick in views and what messages caused that increase.

This can be expanded to include additional marketing channels, or extend deeper into the funnel to include product sales, and more. The important thing is to expand in a methodical way so that you're able to truly understand the data.

Using artificial intelligence and customer journey orchestration together can bring tremendous benefits to your organization. By improving the communication between your marketing platforms, and learning the best ways to reach your customers, this combination can optimize your efforts and create a more valuable customer experience.

digital delight second edition | Greg Kihlström

chapter 2.3
Building an experience measurement platform

"Customer experience is the new marketing."
– Steve Cannon, President & CEO, Mercedes Benz USA

It is estimated that companies in the U.S. are losing as much as $62 billion a year due to poor customer experience alone[5]. This has always been important. But with recent innovations in data storage and marketing technologies, orchestrating, automating and measuring the customer experience is now something that is within reach of more and more companies.

In fact, Grandview Research predicts the customer experience management (CEM) industry itself will grow to $32.49 billion by 2025[6]. This growth is driven by brands' increasing desire to measure the customer experience.

Customer experience doesn't just affect a single marketing channel or department within a company. Thus, unlike many other types of measurement and analytics efforts, building a customer experience measurement plan takes the efforts of many different parts of an organization. I should know; my agency works with clients to create custom customer experience measurement strategies and plans. This process can be divided into five steps, which I'll discuss below:

Ideation

The first phase of the process is where you are free to imagine the possibilities. Create a framework that maps the relationships between points in the customer journey and their associated metrics to your business KPIs and measurements. This is a great time to employ design thinking to build a customer experience around your customer, not around current processes or internal structures.

As you ideate, think about the business areas that the quality of your customer experience affects, such as revenue, the cost to provide your products or services and how profitably you can offer them.

Also, remember to think about how the external customer experience needs to be served by your internal stakeholders. It's not just marketing and customer service that has an impact on how consumers interact with your brand. Think holistically about your organization and every customer touch point or potential operational bottleneck that might affect how your products or services are delivered.

Specification

Turn the framework into a detailed customer experience architecture that incorporates both current and future sources of measurement. This architecture should describe the pathways that customers will take throughout their journeys, the metrics you will be collecting at each step in those pathways and the systems that will be utilized to collect and measure those metrics.

Remember that we also aren't just thinking about one-time purchases or experiences. A true architecture encompasses the customer lifetime and how you get customers to buy, keep buying and recommend others to buy.

This often means that you need to look at a customer experience at two different levels. The first would be the full customer lifetime, which might include multiple purchases and how they interact with your product or service over time. The second would be a more micro view of an individual purchase or interaction. By looking at both levels, you are able to see opportunities, inconsistencies and other needs along the way.

Design

In this step, you turn the architecture into a system design that incorporates the processes, people, data and technology that are required in order for the system to work. Remember, this isn't just about connecting APIs together. To truly measure customer experience, you need to think holistically about how your system will function and work with a combination of human and machine components, and living in the online and offline worlds.

This means that you will be thinking of things in three ways:
- Data collection and analysis, or the tools and systems that help you measure the customer experience along the way
- Listening and activation, or the way that technology and processes respond to customers throughout their journey, and how they are built

to notify teams within your organization when customer assistance is needed
- Operational support, or the internal processes, teams and methods your organization uses to ensure that customers are supported and that issues and requests are handled properly and by the right groups within your company

Implementation

Once the system is designed, you need to build it. Again, this is a series of technical steps and organizational changes to process and procedure which extend across many departments and functions within an organization. Depending on the size and breadth of your operations, this can take several weeks to several months.

Your system will include software, people and processes all working together. Building your customer experience measurement platform with agile methodologies in mind will help you build it more efficiently. The agile sprint-based approach will allow you to more quickly identify areas for improvement, or highlight areas in the process that might have been overlooked and need further attention.

Optimization

The final step in the process is ongoing once you launch. Once the system is implemented, you are live in the market, and it is now time to really begin the work of providing great customer experience. No measurement system should be considered final, regardless of how much planning went into it. Employ agile processes to iterate and improve both your measurement methods as well as the results you get from your measurement. Successful organizations understand that moving beyond the siloed measurement of individual channels, tactics or customer actions provides a win-win.

Customers benefit from a more seamless experience with your products and services, and your internal processes and systems are more aligned with revenue-driving activities.

digital delight second edition | Greg Kihlström

An optimal customer experience measurement platform can make the difference between a general idea of the quality of your customer experience and a true understanding of how consumers interact with your products and services, and how you are performing over time.

chapter 2.4
Experience orchestration

*"Our greatest asset is the customer!
Treat each customer as if they are the only one!"
– Laurice Leitao*

This chapter primarily discusses orchestration as it relates to customer experience, but many of the same principles apply to employee experience orchestration.

There are many tangible benefits of mapping your customer's journey, including improved efficiency within your internal operations and better end results for sales. Increasingly, marketers are turning to automation, personalization and artificial intelligence (AI) to enhance the customer experience within that journey.

Through these efforts, I am seeing marketers experience great results, as customers are more likely to purchase more from a brand due to a great customer experience[7]. Furthermore, 44% of consumers say they are more likely to buy a product if their experience is personalized[8].

At my agency, we work with our clients to map out their customer journeys as part of any marketing engagement. Throughout this process, we look for ways AI and personalization can contribute meaningfully. Many factors lead to our recommendations, including the availability of information that can be personalized, the ability of the client to create content variations for customization and the types of connections available between systems using application programming interfaces (APIs) or other methods.

Whether you've already defined your customer journey or you are just getting started, here are some tips on how to improve your return on investment (ROI) by incorporating AI and automation.

Define your customer journey

The first step is to create an outline or map of your customer journey. In most cases, you will have more than one, just as you have more than one type of customer, though they may share similar steps in the process.

While the individual details may vary, the process follows the same overarching steps:

- **Awareness:** Your customers are starting to discover the problem they are trying to solve and need help to define it.
- **Consideration:** Your customers are trying to decide which company or product to use to solve their problem.
- **Decision:** A conversion is made in the form of a purchase, subscription or another type of "sale."

- **Advocacy:** A customer is now in a position to serve as a referral or a reviewer in the form of word-of-mouth marketing.

Once you've defined your customer journey, you will undoubtedly have several points in it that require solutions that need to be tailored to the individual consumer or company. Remember that your customers are more responsive when you have identified a need that directly relates to them and you provide a solution to their challenge.

Automation and AI, such as chatbots and personalized content, can be very helpful here, as these tactics combine consumers' increasing desire for instant answers and asynchronous communication, and can often save brands time and money once implemented.

Identify the steps where automation will provide the greatest benefits

Once you have defined your customer journey, you can determine the points in which adopting AI and automation make the most sense and will provide the biggest ROI. One way to help with this is to understand where your internal staff and resources are unable to keep up with the demand and/or where a data-driven approach to supplying your customers with answers to their individual questions is needed.

Don't pick tools first and then try to find a way to use them. Instead, first identify the problems you want to solve, and then find the best and most appropriate software and solutions to make your customers' lives easier. With a clearer idea of where you can best implement automation and personalization, you can pick the tools that best fit your needs.

The following are just a few ideas of how you can implement a more intelligent tool set within your customer experience:

- Automated emails based on users' browsing or shopping behaviors to provide support, upsell or cross-sell

- Personalized website content based on location or customer type
- Chatbots that help users navigate your support documentation or frequently asked questions (FAQs)
- Monitoring social media for product mentions and automating responses based on sentiment
- Programmatic ad buying based on behavior or other factors

There are many more methods you can incorporate, but these are some of the ways marketers often get started. Remember, the goal of adopting tools that personalize and automate is to move your customers through the sales funnel more easily and naturally. Pick the times and moments that often have the most friction so that you can see the best and most immediate results. There are considerations to be made as you move forward. You need to ensure that automation will improve the customer experience and not cause more frustration. For instance, does your chatbot application have access to all of the information it might need to fully assist a customer? Thorough testing will help ensure that automated additions to your customer journey make things easier and more effective.

Optimizing your customer journey can lead to happier customers that get what they need and remain loyal because you understand how to solve their ongoing needs. Automation and personalization can be keys to improving your customer satisfaction.

While no customer journey can or should be completely automated, strategic use of personalization, chatbots and other AI tactics has the potential to result in dramatic improvements. From increased customer satisfaction to improved sales, these tools can provide a win-win for your organization and your customers.

digital delight second edition | Greg Kihlström

Chapter 2.5
Optimizing the Customer Experience with AI

Please note, this chapter is primarily focused on customer experience, but we discuss employee experience and artificial intelligence in the next chapter.

As data has become more readily available, and the platforms that companies use to store information about prospective and current customers have become more sophisticated, there has been an increased focus on creating, measuring, and optimizing the customer experience using the best available tools.

There have also been incredible advances in the ability to train and utilize machine learning and other types of artificial intelligence to assist multiple functions within an organization. More specifically, there is incredible opportunity to optimize and enhance the customer experience by using artificial intelligence.

Let's explore 3 ways that artificial intelligence can be used to enhance the customer experience, improve loyalty and increase revenue.

Artificial Intelligence Provides Companies with Better Insights About Their Customers

While the growth in sophistication of data collection and analytics has enabled companies to get vastly better insights about their audiences, artificial intelligence can take that much further by analyzing and finding trends and behaviors that would be impossible for humans to find on their own. This provides organizations with much better and deeper insights about their customers which can benefit marketers, sales directors, CIOs, and other key decision makers.

Companies have never had more access to a greater wealth of data. Whether it's about the company operations and finances, to marketing and sales information, or anything in between, companies are sitting on a considerable amount of information. Part of the challenge this provides, however, is that it becomes too much for even a large team of humans to pore through, analyze, and give recommendations on. This is where artificial intelligence and machine learning can play a huge and vital role.

Artificial intelligence can comb through your data and tell you detailed information about your customers' behaviors and find trends that human analysis would be unable to uncover. This allows you to create more actionable user segments, and supports the personalization customers have come to expect.

Artificial Intelligence Provides Customers with More Relevant Communications

With customers' demands for a personalized experience comes an exponential challenge that requires a solution that can create a vast number of combinations of messaging, offers, timing and sequencing for each individual. The most current and potential customers, the greater the challenge becomes.

Artificial intelligence can improve the delivery of these messages by uniquely tailoring the approach. It helps narrow down the right audience for a message and predict where that audience is looking, and when they are looking, so that messages are more effective.

For instance, utilizing exponential technologies such as personalization and marketing automation, requires understanding an individual customer's information and benefits from understanding their intent and place within the buyer's journey. Utilizing AI can help go beyond sending your audience a limited set of customized messages. It can allow marketers to go beyond simple personas and start customizing messaging, creative, and offers on the individual basis.

Artificial Intelligence Provides Better Performance Over Time

Using artificial intelligence and machine learning, insights gained by customer data can be used to build better ML models which improve as more data is added to the system. This means the more customers the AI reaches, and the more information it gathers about each of them, the better the system performance (the more accurately the system caters to its specified audience). This becomes a continuous cycle of improvement.

For instance, similar to the example above where we discussed using AI in order to analyze and understand audience characteristics in order to build better segments or personas, artificial intelligence can also be used to optimize results. By learning about customer behaviors and applying algorithms or machine learning, we can use AI to optimize steps within the customer journey. That could be anything from tailoring messages, to adjusting the sequence of communications.

In order to more effectively reach audiences and increase marketing performance over time, companies are increasingly augmenting their customer experience with artificial intelligence. From initial marketing communications, through the entire customer lifecycle, AI allows the personalization and customized experience that customers have grown to expect.

Chapter 2.6
Optimizing the Employee Experience with AI

"Connect the dots between individual roles and the goals of the organization. When people see that connection, they get a lot of energy out of work. They feel the importance, dignity, and meaning in their job."
-Ken Blanchard

Just as we discussed customer experience in the last chapter, we're now going to focus on the employee experience and artificial intelligence.

Ensuring your employees are engaged and performing well is critical to your organization's success. The ways to achieve this have evolved over the years to the point where there is a large gap in how different companies measure, assess, and determine the health of the employee experience.

While many organizations still use outdated methods like annual employee reviews or engagement surveys, more forward-thinking organizations are tapping into tools that provide more frequent and more valuable information. Artificial intelligence (AI) is helping more and more of these organizations every day.

In addition to its value in external-facing customer experience, artificial intelligence can play an important role in how employees interact, receive notifications, or even perform critical tasks. Let's look at a few ways that artificial intelligence can enhance the employee experience by breaking it down into three categories.

Insights

A key benefit of artificial intelligence is its ability to crunch large amounts of data to find important insights. No other development has helped organizations make use of the amount of information that the big data push from several years back as much as AI and machine learning-based applications.

And while a lot of these insights have been used to learn more about customers in order to drive more sales, a lot can be done to create more productive and happier employees as well.

An example of how AI can help get better insights is the way some organizations are tying together multiple communication and feedback systems and applying natural language processing (NLP) to them in order to more quickly and easily assess employee sentiment.

Automation

AI is incredibly helpful in automating repetitive tasks which employees may find tedious, or which there may be a greater chance of human error. This is a case where artificial intelligence can replace human workers in a good way. Because while people are great at many things, there are certain types of work that machines can simply do better.

Some examples of automation performed by AI can include finding ways to enhance or orchestrate how information or processes work. Much like customer journey orchestration works with external customers, companies can automate how information flows from one system to another internally as well. This means that artificial intelligence can help companies make sure information is seen quicker, and things like employee feedback are able to be utilized more easily.

Personalization

How do you solve the exponential challenge of giving all of your customers a personalized experience? Another thing that artificial does well is to take your data, match it with individual employee's preferences or other contextual information, and create a personalized experience.

Artificial intelligence can help personalize the experience for employees in a number of ways. This can be done by grouping them into segments at very large companies, or offering very specific communications and messaging if needed. Instead of only segmenting by department or title, more intelligent (and interesting) processing can be done based on communication preferences, or interests.

Think of how you could find employees that have certain characteristics that might make them a match for leadership opportunities, or if you could find complementary skillsets amongst your team to put together new working groups. This becomes incredibly important with a workforce that is increasingly geographically diverse, with both work from home policies becoming more common, as well as teams that are spread across cities and countries. AI can help with all of this.

digital delight second edition | Greg Kihlström

Using AI to improve your company's employee experience enables you to utilize technology in a way that is meaningful and measurable to this critical part of your business. With good insights, the ability to automate previously cumbersome processes, and a focus on making the employee experience more personal, artificial intelligence can serve your business, and your employees, well.

chapter 2.7
Chatbots, CX & EX

"Innovation needs to be part of your culture. Customers are transforming faster than we are, and if we don't catch up, we're in trouble."
— Ian Schafer

Chatbots are increasingly being used by companies to engage with their customers. In fact, it has been reported that 8 in 10 companies[9] have already adopted them or are planning to do so by 2020. This points to fast growth in the market. In fact, 15% of consumers[10] have interacted with a chatbot in the last 12 months, and this number will undoubtedly grow at a quick pace over the coming months.

There is still ground to cover, however, in helping customers become more comfortable with using artificial intelligence for customer support. According to a study by PointSource[11], 54% of survey respondents would still prefer to talk to a real person, with one primary cause for concern being that they feel the artificial intelligence won't understand or might make a mistake.

Chatbots have come a long way, however, and an example of one used to great success is Dom from Domino's Pizza[12]. Introduced in 2016 by the international restaurant chain, Dom allows customers to order their favorite pizza via twelve different methods, including Facebook Messenger, text and Google Home.

Domino's has been successful for several reasons. First, they've made Dom accessible virtually anywhere, from any device. Second, they imbued him with personality. Try chatting with him and he may crack a cheesy (pun intended) joke. Finally, it's unbelievably easy to use, with the ability to order your favorite pizza via simply texting a pizza emoji.

More and more companies are beginning to use chatbots to assist their customers in user-friendly ways. But is your brand ready to utilize a chatbot? Based on my experience, there are several reasons to explore using artificial intelligence and chatbots in your customer service efforts.

You need to offer 24/7 support

A common reason a company makes the decision to start utilizing chatbots is to offer off-hours support in situations where customers have questions around the clock. Staffing customer service or technical support in these situations can be quite costly, particularly for smaller companies.

One of the tangential benefits of doing this is that it allows brands to ease into chatbot adoption during certain hours of the day. You may soon find that your chatbot saves your team a lot of time and effort and choose to start using it 24 hours a day.

Remember, however, that you will need to put in place a robust support system for your chatbots if you choose to adopt them as a full replacement for your current customer service team.

Your customers (and employees) have a lot of common questions

Any company that has frequent customer support needs can have a lot of people who are essentially asking the same thing, albeit in their own words. This is a big drain on your customer service team when a chatbot can interact and answer these queries quickly and easily. This is also a major step up from the classic frequently-asked questions (FAQs) section of a website, or even a technical support forum, because it's interactive in real time, personalized, and it doesn't ask the user to search through a myriad of lists and answers to other irrelevant questions.

What's better, your chatbot can "learn" over time and become more helpful as new questions are asked. There are several benefits to this, such as easily having metrics about the types and volume of specific questions over time and ensuring standardized ways of answering and solving consumers' problems.

Employees have similar issues as well, and may not feel comfortable "bugging" their HR team, or even their managers with every little question they might have. Chatbots work well for cases like this.

It's difficult for your customers to navigate to the correct place to take specific actions

The answers to common questions can often take a consumer from an informational website to an e-commerce page to place or check on an order, or to other locations or systems. The larger the organization, the more systems and integrations might be required to assist your customers.

With a little guidance and setup from your team, your chatbot can easily guide a consumer to the right place to take an action, such as paying a bill, checking on the status of an order, answering a technical support question or any other queries. They can also be helpful when user accounts are required to access systems and your customers have problems with their customer logins, passwords or other data.

These things might take a customer service representative a lot of time and specific knowledge to solve, but artificial intelligence can access multiple systems quickly and securely and help customers in near real time.

While there are several great reasons to use chatbots, there are also factors to consider before adoption. In order to successfully adopt chatbots, you need to be able to guide them quickly and easily to the correct place to find information. If you don't have a consistent method of organizing and updating the information for a chatbot to access, you may run into issues getting consistent results. As great as artificial intelligence can be at learning where to find relevant information, you need to give it an organized structure within which to work and grow.

The adoption of chatbots as part of your customer experience strategy can be beneficial to your business; however, if you have doubts, do some research and see how your customers respond to a limited test. With many frameworks and applications already in place, it is surprisingly easy to create your own.

Remember that you can start small with limited adoption on certain channels or by using the technology to solve specific challenges your customers may face. From my perspective, we are really just starting to see the beginning of chatbot adoption, so it is a good time to start exploring.

Chatbots and EX

For those of you more involved with employee experience than customer experience, you should also be paying attention to the use cases for chatbots.

For instance, at an enterprise where it can take 4-5 different systems just to get onboarded, wouldn't be great to have a single place that you, as a new employee, could go to ask questions?

This makes enough sense that companies are starting to use this feature for employees, not just customers. For instance, VMware's Workspace ONE platform, utilizing a feature called Intelligent Hub which leverages IBM Watson, integrates a chatbot feature into it that greatly streamlines the process of asking anything from a simple to a more complex question in an organization you may be brand new to.

chapter 2.8
Customer loyalty programs & CX

"Loyal customers, they don't just come back, they don't simply recommend you, they insist that their friends do business with you."
– Chip Bell

Please note, this chapter primarily focuses on customer experience, though as always, there are some lessons that can be applied to the employee experience as well.

It is well-understood that acquiring a new customer can be significantly more expensive than keeping an existing one. For instance, recent research by Monetate found that an e-commerce customer who has had one previous shopping experience with a company is over three times more likely to convert again versus a brand new visitor, and customers who have bought multiple times are over five times as likely to convert again[13]. It stands to reason then that customer loyalty programs can be incredibly valuable to any organization with repeat customers.

Loyalty programs are effective at retaining customers by preventing them from turning to the competition. These programs can also maximize the lifetime value of a customer by offering incentives to spend more and buy more often.

Successful customer loyalty programs are win-wins for brands and consumers. They bring additional recurring revenue to the company and make customers happy with perks and rewards. All this adds up to a better customer experience, which can bring better returns.

With so much competition today, one significant challenge is to remain front and center and demonstrate the value of your customer loyalty program.

The average consumer, according to Bond Brand Loyalty[14], belongs to about 14 loyalty programs but uses less than half of those regularly.

One of the things I'm often tasked with doing at my agency is finding new and better ways brands can meaningfully interact with customers. Let's look at three ways customer loyalty programs can enhance the customer experience and create a more active customer base that spends more and buys often.

Personalization and the customer journey

Customer loyalty programs provide an excellent method of using relevant information to personalize the customer journey. Think about it: You already have your customers' information and preferences, and they are incentivized to provide you with more information as long as it can be translated into tangible benefits you can tie to your loyalty program.

Consumers respond well to personalization. In fact, research reveals a customer is eight times more likely to be satisfied with a customer loyalty program if they're very satisfied with how personalized it is to them[15]. There are some very interesting ways that companies are using personalization to enhance the customer experience. For instance, Sephora's Beauty Insider loyalty program stores eye color and skin tone information along with other preferences so it can easily make tailored product recommendations. This makes a big difference in the company's ability to reach customers with relevant information and offers.

Even if your customers aren't providing you with information as detailed as Sephora's customers do, you can still have a big impact on providing relevant content and offers by tracking order history, current service subscriptions and your customers' locations. Demonstrating that you understand your customers and their individual habits and needs can go a long way in making your loyalty program successful.

Make the customer experience easier

Another benefit of a good customer loyalty program is that it streamlines the buying process. Since loyalty programs collect important information from customers, it is a natural fit to store payment information so your customers can quickly make purchases and upgrades.

For instance, Nordstrom Rewards members can browse online and then pick up at the store, thus making it easier to shop and purchase. Starbucks lets you order drinks ahead of time with its app and collect and redeem points in real time. This is a great benefit for loyal Starbucks customers who don't have time to wait in long lines for a cup of coffee.

Because member information is stored already, it can significantly reduce any barriers to making a seamless transaction. You can apply this to your own customer experience in simple ways, such as auto-populating shipping or billing information, providing multiple methods of ordering (via mobile, desktop or even social media) and remembering what a customer ordered previously so they can easily add it to their shopping cart.

Creating customer delight

Finally, a key component of customer loyalty is in finding ways to engage and delight customers. In a crowded market, it's not enough to simply have good customer satisfaction; you need to make them ecstatic and willing to tell others about you. Customer loyalty programs have the ability to do that if done well.

Marriott Rewards members, for example, can check into their room online and even use the mobile app as a room key. It might seem like a small thing, but sometimes conveniences like that can make all the difference between customer satisfaction and customer delight.

Amazon Prime is also a good example for a few reasons. Amazon has created a program that makes paying for and receiving things from the company easier with free shipping, and they've added livestreaming of TV shows, movies and music as well — and customers are willing to pay extra to be a part of this program and receive these perks.

You can create customer delight by employing similar methods. Make the process of buying things or contacting you easier by paying attention to the devices and channels your customers prefer. Don't be afraid to try something new to see what works.

With all the competition out there, brands need a way to stand out while fitting in with their customers' lifestyles. Customer loyalty programs can help brands set themselves apart from the competition while creating a dedicated customer base. Using the right tactics in creating your program can have a measurable, meaningful return on sales and retention.

digital delight second edition | Greg Kihlström

Part 3: Measure

"People don't always remember what you say or even what you do, but they always remember how you made them feel."
– Maya Angelou

"People leave when they don't feel appreciated. That's why we've made recognition a really high value. Our business is people-capability first; then you satisfy customers; then you make money."
- David Novak, CEO of YUM! Brands

chapter 3.1
Where to start with experience measurement

"The first step in exceeding your customer's expectations is to know those expectations." – Roy H. Williams

In order to create a great experience, we need to be able to measure our current ones in order to understand where improvement is needed. Furthermore, once enhancements are made, they need to be monitored for continual improvement.

While this chapter primarily discusses the customer experience, many of the principles and ideas apply just as much to the employee experience as well.

Measuring the customer experience is definitely not as simple as measuring the results of a single tactic such as a website, email marketing campaign or in-store sales. The big challenge with measuring customer experience is that it needs to take into account all of your touch points. The opportunity is worth it, though, as it can show you how small improvements in specific points in the journey can make a huge difference.

But where should you start? In my experience working with many clients looking to improve their customer experience, once a measurement effort is able to launch, no matter how small, it makes a huge difference in the long-term success of the effort. Let's now discuss four things to do to get started in measuring your customer experience that will set you up for success.

Pick an achievable first goal

You can't do everything all at once. In fact, even if you have the time and resources, it's advisable to start relatively small and achieve some early learnings and quick wins.

You could choose a business area with obvious opportunity or a customer segment that can drive significant value. Your data and insights might identify a specific product, service line or audience group that is particularly profitable and increasing in its engagement with your brand. Using one of these as a starting point can be a good way to prove the value of customer experience optimization.

You could also determine where customers are most often leaving for your competitors, and focus on a particular point in the customer journey that needs the most improvement. For instance, is the disconnect between steps in a purchase process too cumbersome? Is it too difficult for someone to repeat a previous online order? Where are the points of friction that make it challenging for your customers to buy more from you?

Focus on one of those as a starting point so you can see the benefit of your efforts quickly.

The other thing to keep in mind is that, particularly for larger organizations, you will probably want to focus your initial plans on a smaller set of customers and/or product lines anyway in order to not create a project that is so large and sweeping in scope that it risks endless delays due to the complexity of changing the way the entire organization does business. By successfully rolling out measurement of a discrete set of target customers, you can then apply your learnings from that initial pilot project to future initiatives.

Define a methodology

After defining your first steps, you need to determine how you will measure success and how you will report on them.

Timing: Make sure you understand what time increments make the most sense based on the purchase cycle. Does monthly, quarterly, year over year or comparing previous periods make the most sense?

Personas: Clearly identify which personas you are measuring against and ensure they have been thoroughly defined.

Accuracy: Ensure you are able to accurately gather data and metrics from each step in the journey and that you are able to determine the sequence of their interactions in order to tell which channels move someone from one step in the process to the next.

Testing: Look at how you are conducting A/B or multivariate tests and how this affects your reporting. Also, keep in mind what reporting frequency makes the most sense for you and your organization.

Build the system

Once you have defined the requirements and determined your methodology, you need to build and connect your system. Most organizations have multiple systems that need to be more fully integrated in order to implement a measurable customer experience.

This will potentially require some custom software development or at least some API integrations between systems and data sources. Make sure you have the buy-in from all necessary parties before you start an effort like this. It may involve systems that different departments or divisions within your organizations are using frequently.

Measure and optimize

Since you've defined your key performance indicators previously, all that is now needed is a way to pull all of the associated metrics into a common platform or report in order to measure your progress.

You might also need some tools to chart or map your success, such as reporting tools that allow multiple data inputs. You can separate your CX measurement into three categories:

Indicators

This includes interaction-based metrics like website visits, social media follows, email opens and other things that indicate a user is interested in the content, offer or product/service you are selling. What did the customer do? These metrics are most likely the easiest to understand because they are generally what marketers are tracking and measuring. They consist of things like product page visits, social media follows or traffic to stores.

Performance

This includes how easily and effectively the process is to generate an outcome. When the customer performed the action, what was the experience like? Did they wait a long time or have to go through many steps? Did they require a phone call or online chat in order to complete the task?

Outcomes

This most closely maps to your overall business and marketing objectives. These are the things you ultimately want customers to do, such as purchasing a product, renewing their membership or recommending a colleague to use your service. What actually occurred as a result of the customer's action?

With the increased focus on customer experience and its optimization, the successful organization will build methods, processes and collections of tools to measure, report and analyze CX. This is a critical step in the process and one that is ultimately responsible for its improvement.

chapter 3.2
The four categories of experience metrics

"I like to listen. I have learned a great deal from listening carefully. Most people never listen."
– Ernest Hemingway

We live in a world of big data, where endless amounts of information can be stored in the cloud at an ever-decreasing cost per byte of storage. While this may sound great to any data-driven marketer, the blessing of cheap storage and increasingly simple API connections between data sources can quickly enough turn into a curse of too much information and not enough time to sort through it all.

In order to overcome this, it is important to choose the right experience metrics. Part of this means that you need to choose data and performance calculations that are critical to your business key performance indicators (KPIs). In order to do this, it's important to take into account all of the types of metrics available in order to get a more holistic picture.

For instance, many of my CX clients are marketers and others focused on customer experience. Thus, many of the metrics and data sources they are dealing with on a daily basis are marketing-driven. Whether they are indicators like website traffic or social media engagement, or conversion statistics on sales or registrations, solely looking at one type of data doesn't give you a comprehensive view of customer experience.

A good experience metrics system includes the following four components that span an entire organization, which we'll review in detail below. While much of the discussion centers around customer experience, most of the ideas and principles also apply to employee experience.

Operational metrics

We will start with the broadest and perhaps most complex type of metric. Operational metrics are the events and actions that happen to customers across their journeys and during their interactions, regardless of the channel (website, phone call, email, social media), or specific department (sales, customer services, accounting) they might be interacting with.

For example, operational metrics can often include some of the best performance-related measurements of what it's truly like to be a customer. How long does it take an insurance customer to go through an entire registration or enrollment process when it might span multiple departments and systems? Or, what is the average resolution time for a customer who calls to complain about their high-speed internet being unavailable?

For employees, operational metrics could include how productive they are (measured in a variety of ways), how their devices are performing (or if they need a replacement), as well as many other metrics.

Analyzing operational metrics can often be the best way to uncover cracks in a business process or disconnects between different teams because they often span disciplines and departments.

The biggest challenge with operational metrics is that, because they often span multiple systems, teams, and potentially even categorization of data, it can often be the most difficult to implement a way to track them.

Subjective metrics

Subjective metrics demonstrate the perceptions that a customer has about what happens and the effect this has on their overall experience and intent. They are often measured either immediately after, or closely following a transaction such as purchase, customer service inquiry, or other interaction with a brand. Their aim is to capture a customer's feelings and impressions as close to "in the moment" as possible.

For example, the Net Promoter Score (NPS) is a great way to measure a customer's subjective opinion about their experience. By utilizing a simple set of questions, companies can measure consumers' feelings about an interaction or process, and compare those in the aggregate to relative timeframes. Understanding year over year (YoY) or even quarter over quarter (QoQ) trends in your NPS can highlight how changes and modifications in your customer experience have effected customer satisfaction.

With employees, the Employee Net Promoter Score (eNPS) provides similar measurements. You might also have other ways to measure engagement or motivation in addition to eNPS.

Subjective metrics are relatively easy to measure, with many simple survey tools readily available to do so.

While not the only indicator of your customers' satisfaction, they are extremely useful information that is easily gained. They shouldn't, however, be used as the only measure of success because they can often be an immediate emotional reaction to an experience. Mixing them with more objective metrics like the others discussed gives the most comprehensive view.

Behavioral metrics

The actions that customers take as a result of their experience and perceptions are defined as behavioral metrics. Unlike subjective metrics, these are objective and observed by either built-in or proprietary reporting platforms on channels that customers interact with. They can range from digital platforms like email communications, to other more offline systems such as call center tracking.

For example, website analytics are a great way to measure customer behavior on that channel. By measuring both individual behavior, as well as behavior of users as a whole, companies can quickly and easily get a good understanding of what customers really do when presented with choices.

Employee behavioral metrics operate similarly, and can often be easier to measure since employers have greater access to what those who work for them are doing on a daily basis, if not on a more granular level. Access to information, applications, documents, and other measurements can tell an organization how engaged and productive an individual may be.

Behavioral metrics are relatively easy to measure, though are often measured in the aggregate, and not on a customer-by-customer basis. There is value in measuring both, but companies should strive to get as much individual customer metrics as possible to truly analyze individual experiences and pathways.

Business metrics

We will end with the type of data most clearly give us a sense of the health of an organization and how well we are executing our strategy. Business metrics can be defined as how customer actions impact your business strategy and goals

For example, business metrics would measure the number of new car buyers over the course of a year, or the number of marketing qualified leads (MQLs) that become sales qualified leads (SQLs) per quarter.

Similar to operational metrics, business metrics can often span disciplines and departments, but are incredibly valuable to an organization. This is simply because business metrics are the most directly tied to financial performance of the company.

For employee experience, business metrics could be things like employee retention, which can deeply affect the bottom line. The cost of replacing an employee can vary from 1/3 to nearly 200% of their salary[16].

A diverse set of experience metrics will give your organization a more comprehensive understanding of where critical issues are, where there is room for improvement, as well as where you currently successful. Utilizing the four types of metrics discussed above in a comprehensive experience measurement system will give you the best possible view of the performance of your CX and EX.

digital delight second edition | Greg Kihlström

chapter 3.3
Choosing the right metrics to measure your experience

"Customer service is the experience we deliver to our customer. It's the promise we keep to the customer. It's how we follow through for the customer. It's how we make them feel when they do business with us."
– Shep Hyken

The value of optimizing your customer and employee experience is clear to most companies. Increasing loyalty, reducing customer service costs, and increasing revenue growth from retained customers, as well as reducing employee turnover, and increasing employee productivity are a few big reasons, in addition to many others.

While it may be easier to come to the conclusion that you *should* measure your experience efforts, a more difficult task is to decide exactly *what* you should measure. To do this, you need to determine what you want your measurement to achieve.

We won't discuss specific metrics in this chapter, because that can be completely dependent on the type of business you belong to, as well as the nuances of your customer experience. But as you'll see, some general rules apply, regardless of the specifics.

Let's explore four primary objectives that your experience measurement metrics should accomplish. We will be referring directly to customer experience a lot in this chapter, but keep in mind that many of the same ideas and principles apply to employee experience as well.

Directly align to your organization's key performance Indicators (KPIs)

First and foremost, if your measurement of experience isn't aligning with your core business KPIs, it will never be truly successful. It is vitally important that you are measuring the right things and asking the right questions at the right time.

In this way, this is definitely about quality over quantity. Make sure you align your experience metrics with the financial and business performance measurements that others in your organization are both familiar with but also responsible for. When you are aligned in this way,

A simple example of this would be to align your measurements and comparisons with your company's reporting schedule. For instance, if you are responsible for quarterly reports on your CX or EX performance, ensure that your measurements and comparisons allow a quarter-over-quarter (QoQ) comparison. You will most likely choose to also measure in other increments as well.

A more complex example of this would be to measure the amount of time that your customers spend at certain points in their customer or employee journey. Particularly when these points in the experience require either specific employees or specific software systems to interact with customers. Looking at key intersections where customer or employee satisfaction and discrete employee roles or software occur can show you how well (or how poor) individual components of your customer experience are performing.

Accurately quantify the quality of the experience

Another key aspect of your CX measurement should be to track and analyze customer interactions and their perceptions of your brand, products and services as they interact throughout the customer journey.

For EX measurement, you will want to do something similarly, by regularly measuring engagement and sentiment, as little things can often shift perceptions and being able to see and respond quickly can make a huge difference.

The best way to do this in a repeatable and scalable way is to try to turn what can often be qualitative, or more subjective opinions expressed by your customers, into more quantitative data.

For example, utilizing Net Promoter Score (NPS) for customers and Employee Net Promoter Score (eNPS) for employees is a great way to do this. Through some relatively simple methods, the NPS allows organizations to objectively track customer satisfaction. Better yet, being able to track changes to this over time give you insights into what is working and what can be improved.

Definitively provide intelligence to make better decisions

What good are the best insights in the world if they don't give you information that can inform your next best actions? As you are defining your experience measurement, think of the questions that need to be answered in order to assess whether your platforms are performing as intended.

If you are able to demonstrate that your customer experience measurement is giving you actionable insights, you will be able to prove the value of an experience-driven approach to business improvement.

For example, choose metrics that help you inform you and your teams' decisions about the journey your customers take as they navigate the customer experience you've created. This could include testing the types or amount of steps that are required to complete an action such as registration or purchase.

Must be agile and able to iterate and optimize
Finally, your experience measurement must be adaptable. As new opportunities, technologies arise, or you add new products and services as an organization, your measurement must be able to keep up. This means leveraging where you currently are and enabling you to

grow and evolve over time to exactly where you want to go.

For instance, my agency helps our clients think through this by teaching agile approaches to planning and road mapping systems such as experience measurement systems, and it helps everyone think in a way that accounts for the potential unknown.

For instance, if you pick metrics and measurements that are only available on a specific software platform and you know that eventually your organization might outgrow it, you should try to find a way to measure things in a way that, even in the future you'll have an "apples to apples" comparison.

The exact metrics you choose to measure will depend on your specific business, but the way that you choose them will be successful if you follow the above guidelines. Remember that it's more important to choose the *right* metrics than to try to track everything.

digital delight second edition | Greg Kihlström

Chapter 3.4
The ROI of Great Employee Experience

"I think when people say they dread going into work on Monday morning, it's because they know they are leaving a piece of themselves at home. Why not see what happens when you challenge your employees to bring all of their talents to their job and reward them not for doing it just like everyone else, but for pushing the envelope, being adventurous, creative, and open-minded, and trying new things?"
-Tony Hsieh

Employee experience (EX) is an increasing priority among companies of all sizes for obvious reasons. With a competitive job market, continual disruption in established industries, and a growing shift in salaried workers into the gig economy, finding ways to keep employees engaged and happy in their positions is a commonsense approach to reduce turnover and motivate employees to do their best work.

While this sounds like common sense, most organizations need more practical justifications to invest in enhancing EX. This means finding the return on investment (ROI) in employee experience initiatives. My agency works with companies of all sizes to find the best and most meaningful methods to do this. We will discuss several of these in the article below.

Tangible benefits of great employee experience

The best way to show return on investment on EX is to use metrics that are easily measured. Here are some of the more concrete and measurable returns on great employee experience.

Let's start with **increased employee retention.** According to TLNT, replacing an employee can cost an organization anywhere from 30% of an entry level salary to 400% of a senior executive's salary. That's a compelling reason to invest in improved employee experience.

Greater productivity is more easily measured in some organizations versus others, but it is important to every organization. According to Gallup, there is a confirmed connection between engaged employees and an increase in productivity. Engaged employees are most often those who experience a superior EX.

Increased customer satisfaction is another measurable outcome of great employee experience. Customer experience has gotten a lot of attention from organizations, where marketing departments are starting to understand how critical experience is to customer acquisition and retention. But what, you ask, does customer satisfaction have to do with employee experience? At my agency Cravety, we always say that what you get on the inside you get on the outside. In other words, happy employees help create happy customers. You can see this in the example of Chik-fil-A, where an emphasis on employee experience has created a fast food chain that [earns nearly double the per-store sales](#) of its next closest competitor, McDonald's.

Less tangible benefits of great employee experience

The above examples show several ways that my agency has used to demonstrate how an investment in employee experience can directly pay off. Now let's explore a few slightly less concrete benefits that, while more difficult to measure, are still inextricably linked to a highly engaged workforce.

Greater innovation is hard to quantify, but invaluable to any organization. In the section above where we discussed tangible benefits, we mentioned increased productivity as an outcome of improved employee engagement. Another byproduct of engagement that stems from improved employee experience is the creation of better products and services, and better solutions to both internal and external challenges. More engaged employees can be much more empathetic to coworkers and to the customers they service. This allows them to come up with more relevant and often *better* ideas that help a company stay innovative and ahead of the competition.

Easier recruiting is often a reason that companies invest in talent branding initiatives. It is true that any branding effort, internal or external, can often pique interests and capture the imaginations of prospective candidates (or customers). But, as sites such as Comparably or Glassdoor have proven, a great-sounding tagline for your talent brand can fall flat if the actual experience of your employees isn't truly great. Instead, investments in great employee experience with a talent brand to match are a winning combination that provides a more seamless recruiting process and can expand your candidate pool to better candidates.

As you can see, there are many different ways that investments in improved employee experience can pay off. Whether they are more tangible, such as decreased turnover rates, or less directly measurable, such as an increase in innovation,

Chapter 3.5
Consumer-centric Measurement of your Customer Experience

> *Loyal customers, they don't just come back, they don't simply recommend you, they insist that their friends do business with you.*
> —Chip Bell

From its title, you can probably see that this chapter is going to be more focused on CX than EX. As with past chapters, however, there are still some lessons to be learned for employee experience practitioners. Measuring your customer experience takes careful planning, a solid infrastructure, and clearly articulated metrics for success. These metrics are often created by looking at what the business needs, not on how the customer perceives success. We can sometimes get so focused on achieving our business key performance indicators (KPIs) that we can lose site of the central part of CX in the first place: the customer.

Let's look at three criteria you can use to make sure you are keeping the customer first when measuring your customer experience.

Value

The first item concerns how effective the process is, and the value that customers get from the experience. Remember that we're putting the customer at the center of this evaluation, so this is what *they* find valuable in their own terms, not how your organization might define value.

For instance, while your business may treat repeat sales as a primary KPI, customers don't value their experience or relationship with your brand based on how much money they give you. Instead, customer value is based on how well you solve their challenges. Many times, this may be helping them by providing a valuable product or service, but just as often, it may be something less financially tangible. Companies that provide great support, helpful content and tips, and offer something more than a product for sale can build better long-term value with their customers.

Efficiency

We also need to make sure that, in addition to having a valuable experience, our customers are able to quickly and easily accomplish their goals. That could be easily purchasing something, scheduling an appointment, or getting more information.

In other words, we need our customers to get value without difficulty, or with as little difficulty as possible.

For instance, the process that it takes to enroll in a service or purchase a product from your website may involve several steps and involve integration between several systems and departments. How easily someone gets all the way through that process has a huge impact on their overall view of your brand. Even the nicest *looking* presentation accompanied by a terrible user experience can ruin someone's opinion and damage what could be a long-term relationship.

Think about not only the time that it takes to complete things, but how easy you make the process along the way.

Satisfaction

Finally, we need to make sure that the customer feels great about their experience both during and after a task is performed. This is the emotional component of the customer experience. While value and efficiency contribute to satisfaction, there are other factors beyond these that can make a big difference.

While customer satisfaction is often measured using tools like the Net Promoter Score (NPS), having an overall mindset of making customers feel great throughout their experience goes beyond this.

This is where the details matter. The types of communication channels available, the language used on a signup form, and the unexpected perks of being a customer or member drive customer satisfaction to new levels when done well. The area of satisfaction is where brands should strive beyond a successful transaction to instead achieve customer delight.

By keeping your customer at the true center of your CX measurement, you can be successful both as a business and in keeping your customers happy. Measuring and tracking both of these types of KPIs is a better way to ensure your customer experience platform is performing well.

digital delight second edition | Greg Kihlström

Part 4: Optimize

"It's very important to have a feedback loop, where you're constantly thinking about what you've done and how you could be doing it better."
– Elon Musk, Founder of Tesla

"Everyone wants to be appreciated, so if you appreciate someone, don't keep it a secret."
– Mary Kay Ash, founder of Mary Kay Cosmetics

Chapter 4.1
Preparing for experience optimization

"The world hates change, yet it is the only thing that has brought progress."
– Charles Kettering

While the leadership in your organization may all be in agreement that investing in CX or EX is important, they may not always understand the far-reaching implications of an optimization effort. After all, unlike other more siloed efforts such as marketing campaigns recruiting efforts, or IT infrastructure enhancements, customer experience and employee touches nearly everyone in your organization.

In order to ensure there is maximum buy-in, follow through, and mutual understanding of what a successful, holistic experience platform looks like, you need to involve stakeholders from across the organization to get involved. There are several questions to ask as you plan your measurement, which we'll discuss below.

What are all of your customer touchpoints?

Let's start with what might be the most obvious, yet potentially the most time-consuming effort. While you may have an easy time identifying some of the most frequently used customer touchpoint, getting an accurate audit of absolutely every one of them can often be an eye-opening exercise.

For instance, your digital channels will undoubtedly include your website, social media, and email marketing, but what about other tools like Glassdoor, or your address listings used for things like Google Maps? Then you have all of your offline touchpoints. Where are all the points where a customer could need or want to talk with someone on the phone? This could be everything from an initial sale, to billing inquiries, to customer service and complaints. If you have brick and mortar locations, who are all the different people that a customer might interact with? You'll quickly see that this isn't a simple list of a few things, but often a broad list of touchpoints across many mediums.

Another thing to keep in mind is to be realistic about having a full audit of customer touchpoints versus feeling you need so implement all of them into a cohesive platform on day one.

Often, with the clients I work for, we will want to do a full accounting of customer touchpoints, but may start building and measuring in phases by only focusing on a fraction of them, or by those places where there are quick wins available.

What about employee touchpoints?

Similar to the section above, do you have an accounting of all the different touchpoints you have with your employees? Chances are there are quite a few, and they are quite wide ranging, such as:

- Messaging found during the recruiting process
- The choices you give about devices and applications
- The way managers communicate with their direct reports
- Digital communications such as company emails and intranets
- The way meetings are conducted with remote employees

The above is only a small fraction, but you can see how long the list could get for employee touchpoints alone!

How do you share insights with internal stakeholders?

Sometimes the visibility that internal teams have on efforts such as customer or employee experience optimization can make all the difference in their success.

For instance, even if you have a primarily digital methodology to reach customers, do you have a way to report the success or challenges to other internal team members who may have even a tangential relationship to the outcomes? Your customer service team might not be responsible for the user experience of the website, but what is their response time when a support-related inquiry is sent through the site?

The same goes with employees. Technically sending an email to "all staff" doesn't mean that the communication was effective, or even read by "all" or even *most* of the team. The content is important, but so is the medium and channels used to communicate.

Giving a broader team visibility over the success of your experience platform allows them to see both the part that their teams play, as well as can often drive them to have insights about ways to improve processes.

Where should you focus actions?

As I mentioned above under the first point, you should prioritize quick wins and create prioritized backlog of future initiatives. This is often successful when utilizing an agile approach, where tasks are grouped in logical sets and tackled one at a time.

For instance, if the dropoff in customer acquisition is at its steepest decline at a specific point in the buying process, you may want to start optimizing your customer experience there, for a few reasons. First, it's something you already know, so there's an immediate problem to solve. Second, since the buyer's journey is critical to any business, it seems that there will be an immediate return, i.e. more paying customers. Finally, this could be considered a quick win for your customer experience optimization efforts, thus quickly and easily proving the value of your efforts.

The same goes for employee experience. You may have an employee retention issue that is challenging, but have a good understanding that by simply finding the right organizational culture matches from the start, you may have an easier time in the long run. This means that you could focus initially on finding better ways to interview and select the best possible employees before they start working at the company.

After all, not every type of optimization is going to be so easy. It's best to start with one that can more immediately prove the ROI of examining your CX or EX platform.

It should go without saying that you should focus your actions on items that are directly in line with business key performance indicators (KPIs), but often the way you prioritize needs to be more nuanced than that.

By focusing on something where there is either a major bottleneck that could drastically help a process, or by something that will be easy enough to start measuring, we can let some quick wins prove the value of experience optimization to the rest of the organization.

What logistical challenges exist?

Even with the best intentions, there can be roadblocks to even the most strategic efforts within an organization. Understanding what logistical challenges may exist in implementing a far-reaching experience platform and optimization process can mean the difference between short-term success and indefinite delays.

With CX, for instance, if your CRM platform is difficult to integrate with other systems, or if your website is maintained by a third party, understanding what the potential challenges with integrating them are crucial to understand from the start.

By confronting potential logistical or operational challenges head-on, your customer experience platform optimization effort has a much better chance of long-term success. Seemingly mundane details can often derail an operation or indefinitely delay it.

In addition to the items above, some other obvious questions need to go into your planning, such as what your budget is, what KPIs you will use to benchmark success, and other items like that.

Just as important as building the right experience platform or planning how you will measure success with CX or EX, is to make sure that you have a realistic plan to support your efforts. Getting key stakeholders bought in to the process and creating a realistic plan to measure and optimize your platform will enable it to stay successful in the long term.

digital delight second edition | Greg Kihlström

chapter 4.2
Optimizing experience

"We see our customers as invited guests to a party, and we are the hosts. It's our job every day to make every important aspect of the customer experience a little bit better."
— Jeff Bezos

In a busy organization with many competing priorities, it can often be difficult to keep focused on even the most important aspects of keeping a business performing exceptionally. Customer and employee experience platforms often involve many different teams across an organization, and thus it's critical to ensure a "big picture" view is kept. Too often, teams can get too concerned with measurements and performance in their silo within the organization, but truly successful CX and EX platforms are built, measured, and optimized holistically.

This organization-wide approach is best when the measurement criteria are broader than a specific set of channels or actions, but instead focus on operational performance and business-level objectives. Let's now discuss four criteria of a successful experience optimization plan.

Practical

A practical customer or employee experience measurement platform is one that enables maximum value with minimal time and dollars spent maintaining it and keeping it current.

It also means that the metrics, analysis, and insights you get from your measurements are able to inform your business. These need to be return on investment (ROI)-

driven insights you can share with your team and other customer experience stakeholders.

For instance, if the analytics you get from your customer experience platform take hours of processing and crunching in order to get a cohesive report about its performance, it's not practical. The more difficult any platform is to use, the less likely it will be used, which can cause things to quickly fall into disrepair as workarounds are found.

A simple, but classic example of this for CX is how an outdated website will often cause salespeople to make their own PDFs, landing pages, and other workarounds to avoid having to send people to a website that doesn't reflect the current reality. Doing so skews all your numbers, and disrupts an optimal customer experience.

In the world of employee experience, an example is in device and application usage. If companies make it too cumbersome to get important work done, employees will often go to great lengths to find workarounds using devices from home or non-sanctioned applications which cause nothing but headaches down the road when work needs to get reconciled.

Scalable

An experience platform with scalability can keep up with the growth trajectory of your business. Being scalable means that it can handle both a growing external customer base, a growing employee and sometimes hourly workforce, as well as the internal teams that will be operating it.

A scalable experience platform doesn't always have to be able to handle exponential growth. But it needs to be able to handle the fluctuations and changes of your business. This may either be steady growth (whether fast or slow), or it could be massive fluctuations in volume during short periods of time.

For instance, an e-commerce company may experience high volume of all types of customer activity during the holiday shopping season. This includes purchases, returns, and all other types of customer inquiries and complaints. Rapid fluctuations take a different type of scalability than a system for a company's needs which are growing slower and steadier, or with less volatility from month to month or season to season.

Improvable

Similar to being scalable, your experience measurement needs to be able to be modified and added to over time. Where this differs from scalability is that being improvable may mean that existing systems or steps in a process can be modified and optimized without the need to necessarily handle more traffic, inputs, or data storage.

An improvable experience platform is often made to be modular, with distinct parts each playing a role, but seamlessly working with another. This modular approach allows different components, such as tracking or measurement tools to be switched in and out as needs change, or as better components become available.

Another way to make sure your experience platform is made to be improvable is to customize it to your business in a way that is easy for your internal team to modify as needed. This will often require an internal technical team with a broad understanding of the different needs across the organization. While there can sometimes be risks with creating proprietary systems, a mix of proprietary and off-the-shelf systems has worked well for some of the clients I work with.

Your experience measurement must be flexible and adaptive enough to change with the times. While we talked about scalability and improvability, there are many other factors that might need to be modified over time.

An agile experience platform can change with a business as it grows, evolves, and as demand in different areas changes over time. Though we mentioned scalability earlier, this doesn't always involve growth. For instance, in a world of continual disruption of industries and often well-established practices, an agile customer or employee experience platform is able to adapt itself to new platforms, modifications to internal processes, and changes in tactics from marketing, human resources, technology, or customer services teams.

Measuring your customer and employee experience takes a lot of strategy, coordination, and continual optimization but can have huge returns on even slight improvements in consumer and employee satisfaction and retention.

Conclusion
Digital delight

"The key is to set realistic...expectations, and then not to just meet them, but to exceed them – preferably in unexpected and helpful ways."
– Richard Branson

We're fortunate to live in a time when are able to design, observe, and optimize the experience that our customers and employees have, with increasing success. Better tools, easier access to data and measurements, and more sophisticated data processing capabilities all provide building blocks necessary for building an experience platform.

But these tools require creativity and design thinking, deep human (and AI) analysis and insights, and a commitment to making a better experience for customers and employees.

I hope you've found inspiration in the preceding pages, and gotten some both practical and aspirational ideas of how you can create a better experience optimization platform of your own.

It all starts with a clear vision of what customer and employee delight means to your organization. Aligning it with your company purpose and values means it will yield authentic results.

The ultimate goal of delight requires planning, building, measurement and optimization. The ultimate measurement of success is delight. Delight for customers, who keep buying more and tell others about their experience. And delight for employees who stay engaged, productive, and love where they work.

References

[1] Roger L. Martin. "Use Design Thinking to Build Commitment to a New Idea." Harvard Business Review. January 3, 2017.
https://hbr.org/2017/01/use-design-thinking-to-build-commitment-to-a-new-idea

[2] Tom Richey. "Analysis and Synthesis. On Scientific Method." Systems Research. 1991.
http://www.swemorph.com/pdf/anaeng-r.pdf

[3] David Linthicum. "The Value of Data Integration is Pretty Easy to Define." Informatica Blog. November 18, 2016.
https://blogs.informatica.com/2016/11/18/the-value-of-data-integration-is-pretty-easy-to-define/#fbid=3m-7yJV6Wwz

[4] Segment (Press Release). "Segment Survey Finds Consumers Will Spend More When Their Shopping Experience is Personalized, but Most Retailers are Missing the Mark." October 25, 2017.
http://www.marketwired.com/press-release/segment-survey-finds-consumers-will-spend-more-when-their-shopping-experience-is-personalized-2238385.htm

[5] NewVoiceMedia. "Serial Switchers Strikes Again: How the Billion-Dollar Customer Service Problem Prevails." 2019. https://www.newvoicemedia.com/en-us/resources/serial-switchers-strikes-again-us

[6] Grand View Research (Press Release). "CEM Market Size Worth $32.49 Billion By 2025." May 2018. https://www.grandviewresearch.com/press-release/global-customer-experience-management-cem-market

[7] Bruce Temkin. "2017 Temkin Experience Ratings, U.S." March 2017. http://www.temkingroup.com/wp-content/uploads/2017/05/1703_TemkinExperienceRatingsUS_FINAL.pdf

[8] Segment. "The 2017 State of Personalization Report." 2017. http://grow.segment.com/Segment-2017-Personalization-Report.pdf

[9] Business Insider. "80% of Businesses want Chatbots by 2020." https://www.businessinsider.com/80-of-businesses-want-chatbots-by-2020-2016-12?r=UK

[10] Erik Devaney. "The 2018 State of Chatbots Report: How Chatbots Are Reshaping Online Experiences." January 23, 2018. https://blog.drift.com/chatbots-report/

[11] PointSource. "2018 Artificial Intelligence and Chatbot Report: Finding Common Ground Between Consumers and Artificial Intelligence: a Closer Look at Consumers' Current Relationship with Chatbots." 2018. https://digital.pointsource.com/acton/media/21911/2018-artificial-intelligence-and-chatbot-report

[12] Paul Sawers. "Domino's beats Pizza Hut to launch Facebook Messenger bot, but it could be smarter." August 12, 2016.
https://venturebeat.com/2016/08/12/dominos-pizza-bot/
[13] Monetate." A Retention Story: Ecommerce Quarterly Report." 2017. http://info.monetate.com/rs/092-TQN-434/images/EQ12017-ecommerce-report.pdf
[14] Bond Brand Loyalty. "The 2016 Bond Loyalty Report: What's Trending in Loyalty?"
https://info.bondbrandloyalty.com/hubfs/Bond_Brand_Loyalty_2016_Loyalty_Report_Infographic.pdf?t=1512069435103
[15] Bond Brand Loyalty. "The 2016 Bond Loyalty Report: What's Trending in Loyalty?"
https://info.bondbrandloyalty.com/hubfs/Bond_Brand_Loyalty_2016_Loyalty_Report_Infographic.pdf?t=1512069435103
[16] Work Institute. Retention Report 2017. http://info.workinstitute.com/retentionreport2017

www.ingramcontent.com/pod-product-compliance
Lightning Source LLC
Chambersburg PA
CBHW072028230526
45466CB00020B/1125